On December 12, 1937, just four short years before the infamous attack on Pearl Harbor, Japanese planes bombed and sank an American gunboat, U.S.S. *Panay*, in the Yangtze River, deep in the interior of China. This unprecedented action against a neutral power rocked America. Protestations that the attack was accidental did not conceal the true extent of Japanese aggression and worldwide ambitions. The United States began to prepare itself, albeit slowly, for the world war that was sure to come.

PRINCIPALS

OFFICERS OF THE U.S.S. *Panay:*
  Lieutenant Commander James J. Hughes, commanding officer
  Lieutenant Arthur F. Anders, executive officer
  Lieutenant (junior grade) John William Geist, engineering officer
  Ensign Denis H. Biwerse, communications officer
  Lieutenant Clark G. Grazier, medical officer
ADMIRAL HARRY E. YARNELL, commander in chief, U.S. Asiatic Fleet
NELSON T. JOHNSON, American ambassador to China
JOSEPH C. GREW, American ambassador to Japan
GEORGE ATCHESON, second secretary, American embassy, China
JOHN H. PAXTON, second secretary, American embassy, China
FRANK N. ROBERTS, captain U.S. Army, assistant military attaché, China
NORMAN ALLEY, cameraman, Universal Newsreel
ERIC MAYELL, cameraman, Fox Movietone
KINGORO HASHIMOTO, Japanese army colonel
Kiyoshi HASEGAWA, vice admiral Japanese navy
KOKI HIROTA, Japanese foreign minister

The U.S.S. Panay *on her sea trials off Shanghai, one of a new group of American gunboats designed specifically for the famed Yangtze River Patrol and destined to become the subject of an "incident" that would lead to worldwide notoriety. (United Press International)*

A FOCUS BOOK

The Panay Incident,
December 12, 1937

*The Sinking of an American Gunboat Worsens
U.S.-Japanese Relations*

by Joseph B. Icenhower
Rear Admiral, U.S. Navy (ret.)

FRANKLIN WATTS, INC.
845 Third Avenue · New York, New York 10022

The authors and publisher of the Focus Books wish to acknowledge the helpful editorial suggestions of Professor Richard B. Morris.

E
183.8
J3
I25

Maps by Dyno Lowenstein

SBN 531-00992-0
Library of Congress Catalog Card Number: 70-161832
Copyright © 1971 by Franklin Watts, Inc.
Printed in the United States of America
1 2 3 4 5

Contents

The *Panay* Incident

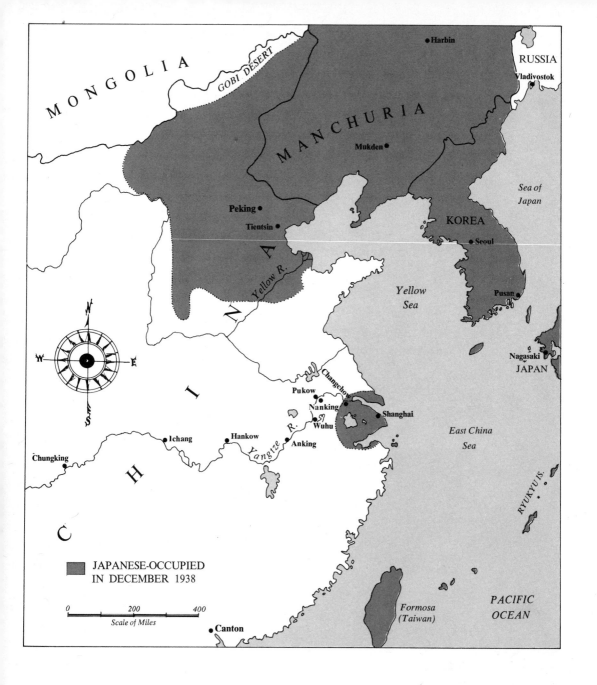

RUSSIA

• Harbin

Vladivostok

MONGOLIA

GOBI DESERT

M A N C H U R I A

Mukden •

Sea of
Japan

Peking •

Tientsin •

KOREA

• Seoul

Yellow R.

Yellow
Sea

Pusan •

Nagasaki •

JAPAN

Changchow

Pukow •
Nanking •

Wuhu •

Shanghai •

East China
Sea

Ichang •

Hankow •

Anking •

Yangtze R.

Chungking •

H

C

JAPANESE-OCCUPIED
IN DECEMBER 1938

RYUKYU IS.

0   200   400
Scale of Miles

PACIFIC
OCEAN

Formosa
(Taiwan)

• Canton

China Setting–The Yangtze Patrol

At the close of the Civil War, in 1866, the United States sent two paddle-wheel steamers to China to protect American citizens and interests in that country. These two ships, the U.S.S. *Monocacy* and the U.S.S. *Ashuelot*, were the first vessels of an incredible little naval force later named the Yangtze Patrol Force, or YangPat. Over the years it grew, and by the time it was made a subdivision of the U.S. Asiatic Fleet after the Spanish-American War, YangPat, although small, was a force to be reckoned with, as numerous semi-independent Chinese warlords soon learned. Yangtze Patrol boats earned for themselves a "can-do" reputation, and it is well that they did, for when the Manchu Dynasty was overthrown in 1911, China became one vast battlefield, with warlord fighting against warlord and all of China pitted against the Western barbarians.

Authority for the United States to operate naval vessels on the inland waters of China was granted under the terms of the Sino-British Treaty of 1858. As a treaty power the United States enjoyed the rights extended by China to Great Britain. Although the upper Yangtze River had no "treaty ports" on its shores, the major powers acknowledged one another's rights to patrol this river as being necessary to protect their citizens and their interests in this turbulent area.

Although deeming it essential to "show the flag" and even to engage Chinese military units on occasion, the United States championed China's rights as an independent nation and sought to maintain an "Open Door" policy with the Asian power. This policy, set forth by John Hay, the American secretary of state in 1899, sought to limit the wholesale division of China by the great nations of the world. It forbade any power the right to extend to its own citizens any preferential treatment with regard to taxes and dues and retained for China the right to collect customs dues and other fees. In general, Hay also hoped to prevent one power from interfering in any treaty port or sphere of influence. The secretary hoped that such limitations would prevent further disruption of China.

Even so the American government had to adopt a practical course of protecting its citizens and interests because the central Chinese government could not, in some instances, and would not in others, exercise adequate control over her military and semimilitary forces. After the turn of the century conditions in China steadily worsened and YangPat experienced ever-increasing demands on its limited force.

Thus during the decade following the overthrow of China's central government, these river patrol boats found themselves extremely busy trying to protect Americans and their interests along the 1,300-mile stretch of the Yangtze from Shanghai to Chungking. This era of fighting saw many bloody battles, although there were few fatalities on the American side. The British also maintained river patrol boats of the same general design and occasionally the two joined forces. One notable cooperative venture occurred when three small British gunboats, with a force that numbered 110 in all, attacked a well-armed Chinese army of 15,000 men. The British suffered numerous casualties and the U.S. destroyer *Stewart* rushed to their assistance. When the American ship reached Hankow with the wounded, she had to use her main battery to blast her way into the city docks.

These years of turbulence were succeeded in the mid 1920's by an even more dangerous period. The danger developed when a Cantonese army under Generalissimo Chiang Kai-shek moved north with fire and sword to purge China of the chaotic warlord enclaves, and

[4]

YANGTZE RIVER GUNBOATS

U. S. S. Oahu Patrolling the Yangtze River

Powerful light draft naval vessels protect American lives, alleviating distress and assisting commerce on the upper Yangtze River. These gunboats penetrate regions over 1300 miles from the sea in a land where transportation and communication is primitive.

A recruiting poster depicts the Yangtze River gunboat U.S.S. Oahu, *sister ship of the* Panay. *(U.S. Navy)*

to spread the philosophy of Dr. Sun Yat-sen's New China Republic. Prodded by their Russian advisers, the Cantonese army commanders initiated a succession of antiforeign harassments against the British, American, Italian, and Japanese interests.

At this time there were numerous American ships operating on the river, as many as twenty on the upper river above Ichang and through the gorges all the way to Chungking. YangPat, now consisting of two minesweepers, an ex-yacht, and four small river gunboats, was augmented by a light cruiser and ten destroyers to patrol the lower reaches of the river. YangPat was thus a potent force and one that kept busy. There were no less than thirty-seven actions or encounters with Chinese military units during 1927–28.

By the following year, the Cantonese had become the Nationalist Chinese forces and some measure of tranquillity descended on the muddy Yangtze River. While anti-Western harassment continued, it was something the British and Americans could live with. But the Japanese, who substantially increased their Imperial Navy in Chinese waters and began to make warlike noises, could not. The Nationalists, much to the surprise of a watching world, did not capitulate to Japanese demands. They did, however, rid themselves of their Soviet advisers, sending the fortunate ones home and saving traveling expenses on the unfortunate by simply shooting them. Then Chiang, in need of both funds and time to consolidate his gains, started to woo the formerly hated British and Americans.

Initial hostilities between the Japanese and Chinese began around Shanghai in 1932. They continued sporadically until 1937 when they erupted into a full-scale, but still undeclared, war.

Japanese army and navy forces struck upriver from Shanghai, meeting surprisingly stubborn resistance from the Nationalist Chinese forces. A war that the Japanese looked forward to completing in months had only reached Nanking, the ancient capital of China, by December, and there still remained much of China to subdue.

As Japan's incursions in China gained momentum, the Japanese military became more and more anti-American, and the Japanese government placed little or no restraint on those who were in favor of making war. While not directly related to any one incident in Sino-Japanese hostilities, these hatreds grew out of the military arrogance of the decade and deep-seated resentment of America's treatment of Asiatics. In 1924 Congress had enacted a law limiting the number of immigrants that could enter the United States. This lim-

[6]

ited number was based on a formula derived from the number of any one nationality then residing in the country. In the case of Japan, however, even though under the formula some two hundred Japanese should have been allowed to enter the United States, Congress chose to exclude *all* Japanese. From this moment on, the possibility of rapport between the two nations seemed very dim.

Even greater stresses on the relations between the two Pacific sea powers were caused by Japan's determination to dominate all of Asia. Above and beyond the concessions granted all treaty powers, Japan insisted on recognition of her "special interests" in China. In 1915 she submitted to a disrupted Sino government her infamous "Twenty-one Demands," designed to give Japan virtual control of China's major functions. The United States vigorously protested the demands and world opinion forced the Japanese to back down on many of them.

Recognizing that naval supremacy in Asia was vital to her projected expansion, Japan determined to increase her already substantial navy. As a result of the Washington Conference of 1921, and the remarkable apathy of Great Britain and the United States, Japan was conceded naval dominance of the northern Pacific and Asian waters. During the London Naval Conference of 1930 she further demanded, and received, certain improvements in naval parities with the Great Powers.

In 1931 Japan occupied much of Manchuria and successfully defied League of Nations censure. Encouraged by Great Britain's refusal to join the United States in contesting this take-over, she hardened her determination to attempt to conrol all of mainland China. Fearing only a combined Anglo-American naval effort, and seeing no firm accord between those two nations, Japan felt free to pursue her designs on China.

[7]

America's sea power made no great gains during the early 1930's but Japan's grew apace. As her war-making capacity increased, military extremists gained control of the government and the nation embarked on a policy of virtually naked conquest. Encouraged by Mussolini's defiance of world opinion in Ethiopia and Hitler's arrogance on the Continent — which checkmated any firm Asian policy by Great Britain — Japan became openly contemptuous of America. By 1937 this contempt was to become apparent in a most dramatic event.

A New Gunboat–The U.S.S. *Panay*

On Saturday morning, December 11, 1937, the U.S.S. *Panay* lay anchored off the Bund at Nanking. This inland city, evacuated by the diplomatic personnel of most countries only recently, was under heavy artillery and air attack by the combined military forces of Japan.

The *Panay*, one of the new group of gunboats built at Shanghai in 1926–27 and designed specifically for the Yangtze River Patrol, was named for an island in the Philippines. She drew slightly more than 6 feet of water forward and aft, and she had a flat bottom similar to a Mississippi stern-wheeler.

The vessel's commanding officer was Lieutenant Commander James J. Hughes. Observing the river from his vantage point on the bridge of the gunboat, Commander Hughes was keenly aware of the critical situation and he mentally reviewed his ship's mission as stated on a bronze plaque in the wardroom. By that statement, the *Panay* was to protect American life and property in the Yangtze River Valley and its tributaries, and also to further American good will in China. As commanding officer he would have a difficult time protecting Americans and their property when the Japanese took the city. And, as far as furthering American good will, the time was hardly propitious.

Virtually all American embassy personnel had gone with Ambassador Nelson T. Johnson when that envoy, at the insistence of the Chinese government, had removed to Hankow. Only a skeleton force remained behind and the *Panay*, acting as a communications center, remained their sole link with the outside world.

Anchored close to the *Panay* were three Standard Oil tankers,

Crew of the U.S.S. Panay *mustered for ship's picture.* Panay's *skipper, Lieutenant Commander James Hughes (center), is flanked by ship's commissioned officers. Behind them stand chief petty officers. Note old-style uniforms of enlisted personnel — blue collars on dress whites. (United Press International)*

Lieutenant Commander Hughes, skipper of the gunboat Panay. *(United Press International)*

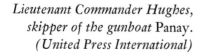

the S.S. *Meihsia*, S.S. *Meiping*, and S.S. *Meian*. Commander Hughes knew, from the anxious queries he had had from their skippers, that they were more than ready to leave, but dared not do so until the *Panay* could escort them.

Just across the muddy river, Commander Hughes could see the fire and smoke rising from the rail center of Pukow, the hub of China's rail network. All week Japanese planes and artillery had pounded these rail yards, indiscriminately killing and wounding Chinese soldiers and civilians alike. If Nanking were to receive the same kind of punishment, he reflected, there would not be too much left of the ancient capital.

Although the *Panay* had shifted her anchorage several times in

The U.S.S. Panay *alongside dock at Nanking on December 12, 1937. City is being shelled by Japanese artillery. (U.S. Navy)*

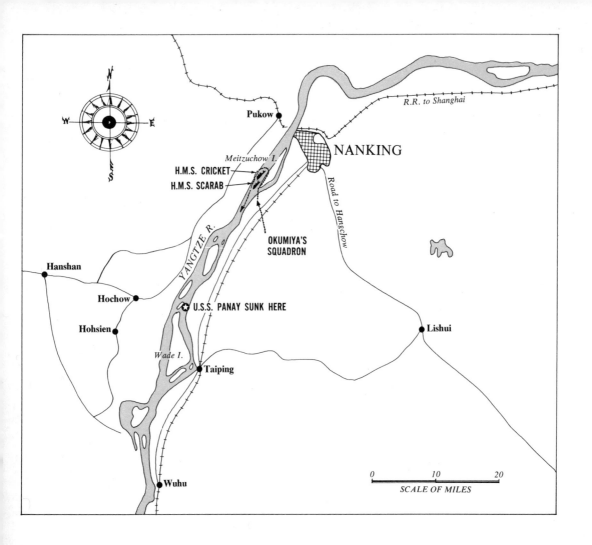

order to get out of the line of Japanese fire, the commander was not particularly alarmed for her safety. The American flag was displayed prominently — both horizontally and vertically — on the ship. On the top deck a huge, 16-foot flag warned Japanese planes that the *Panay* was a U.S. vessel.

[12]

Certainly the *Panay* herself posed no great threat to the Japanese naval and ground forces attacking Nanking. Only 191 feet long and displacing over 500 tons, her armament consisted of two 3-inch guns and ten 30-caliber machine guns. While the ship was under instructions to remain completely neutral in the conflict, the 3-inch guns were covered for another reason. In order to fire them, the watertight hatches and doors had to be opened to obtain ammunition (thus destroying their watertight integrity). As for the 30-caliber machine guns, they could do little more than repel a river pirate attack.

An air view of the American flag prominently displayed aft on the Panay. *(United Press International)*

As Nanking Fell...

Ashore in the embassy compound, Second Secretary George Atcheson, impeccably dressed even during this critical period and every inch the diplomat, sighed as he wiped the lens of his gold-rimmed glasses. The time had come to board the *Panay*. Even more important, it was time to order the few remaining American nationals to leave the doomed city. This would prove difficult, he was sure. One couple had previously refused to leave their property in the city. Even the threat of increased bombing and artillery attacks would fail to move some people. Mr. Atcheson knew he would have a special problem trying to induce the United States cameramen and war correspondents to leave. These intrepid members of the fourth estate were running incredible risks in order to cover the Japanese undeclared war on China.

With one last look around he called his driver and had himself driven to the Italian embassy. A number of newsmen, bombed out of the Hotel Metropolitan on December 1, had accepted the Italians' offer of quarters. The Americans billeted here were about as top-flight a group of war correspondents as any in the world. There was Eric Mayell of Fox Movietone, Norman Alley of Universal Newsreel, Arthur Menken of Paramount News, and Jim Marshall of *Collier's* Magazine. Their hosts at the embassy were Luigi Barzini of *Corriere Della Sera* of Milan and Sandro Sandri of *Il Popolo D'Italia*. Not at the Italian embassy, but somewhere in the bomb-wracked city, were Norman Soong of the *New York Times*, C. Malcolm Mac-Donald of the London *Times*, and Weldon James of United Press.

No one answered Atcheson's hammering on the embassy door although several newsmen had seen him from one of the upper

[14]

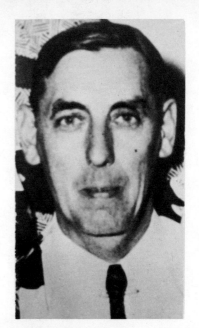

Three of the American newsmen who were aboard the Panay on the fatal day were (right) Eric Mayell of Fox Movietone; (below left) Norman Alley of Universal Newsreel; and (below right) Jim Marshall of Collier's Magazine. (United Press International)

Members of the American embassy staff and news correspondents wait at the jetty in Nanking for the launch that will take them to the Panay. *(United Press International)*

windows. After Atcheson left, however, the newsmen held a hurried conference and decided they had better take their gear out to the *Panay*. The fall of Nanking was obviously not far away.

The gunboat had a launch waiting at the Bund when the American correspondents drove up in Norman Alley's old car. The launch

[16]

had a long trip out to the *Panay*. Commander Hughes had moved the ship farther upstream during the air raid on the Pukow rail yards. Too many stray bombs and artillery shells had been landing close by, and he was also anxious to get the highly explosive tankers out of danger.

Arthur Menken elected to stay behind to cover the fall of the city. He well knew the risks he ran. General T'ang Sheng-chih, in spite of his German advisers' protests, was determined to make a last-ditch stand. If the Japanese encountered really stubborn resistance Nanking could expect little better than an orgy of rape and pillage. Only the Hsiakuan Gate to the city now remained open for refugees to flee and it would soon be closed. Menken knew from experience that the Japanese were notoriously lax in observing the rights of neutrals.

Sandri, Barzini, and Herbert Ros, vice-consul at the Italian embassy, joined the Americans on the Bund. Several messages between Nanking, Hankow, and Shanghai had cut the red tape sufficiently to permit foreign nationals to board the ship. MacDonald, as a Briton, had little difficulty gaining permission to board the gunboat. Captain Frank Roberts, assistant military attaché at the American embassy, J. Hall Paxton, another second secretary, and Emile Gassie, code clerk, completed the embassy group. Two American businessmen, D.S. Goldie of Standard Oil Company and Roy Squires, joined the group. Norman Soong showed up just in time to catch the last trip of the launch — to safety, so he thought, under the Stars and Stripes.

Earlier, midway between Shanghai and Nanking that same bright Saturday, a group of newly arrived Japanese naval pilots were being briefed as to the next day's targets at Nanking. Rear Admiral Teizo Mitsunami's 2nd Combined Air Group had complete control of the air. No fighter opposition was expected and the pilots were

[17]

Army Captain Frank Roberts, military attaché at the American embassy in Nanking, who was aboard the Panay *during the bombing incident. (United Press International)*

informed that the target was to be the city's east gate. The 12th Air Group, one of two, consisted of twelve fighters, twelve bombers, and six dive bombers under the command of Captain Sadatoshi Senda. The second air group was the 13th, under the command of Captain Morihiko Mike, and contained twelve bombers, twelve fighters, and twelve dive bombers. These two groups formed the 2nd Combined Air Group.

The Japanese air commanders received their target designations and air intelligence from Lieutenant Commander Takeshi Aoki, liaison officer on Lieutenant-General (Prince) Asaka's staff. Asaka commanded all army forces attacking Nanking. The Japanese had learned of the U.S. Navy and merchant ship movements from Admiral Harry Yarnell, commander in chief of the U.S. Asiatic Fleet, aboard his flagship, the cruiser U.S.S. *Augusta*, and from the

United States consulate, both in Shanghai. Likewise, the Japanese army and navy had received word this Saturday morning of the *Panay's* anticipated movement upriver.

At 5 P.M. Lieutenant Commander Hughes gave his executive officer, Lieutenant Arthur F. ("Tex") Anders, orders to get under way. Japanese artillery shells were falling perilously close, not only to the American gunboat but also to the three Standard Oil tankers. One chance hit on a tanker would probably turn it into a roaring

Admiral Harry E. Yarnell, commander in chief of the U.S. Asiatic Fleet, aboard his flagship, U.S.S. Augusta. *(United Press International)*

inferno. The ships anchored again about 12 miles north of the doomed city.

George Atcheson, in his official report to the secretary of state, Cordell Hull, claimed that Japanese artillery shells followed the ship and her convoy as they proceeded upriver. The substance of this was vouched for by Colonel Lovat-Fraser of the British embassy, and Dr. Rosen, secretary of the German embassy. Both of these men were with the British gunboats H.M.S. *Cricket* and H.M.S. *Scarab* which were then in the same area.

This movement upstream of the four American vessels was also reported to the U.S. State Department offices in Shanghai, Peking, Hankow, and to the American ambassador in Tokyo. The latter officer was requested to notify the Japanese government and the U.S. secretary of state in Washington. All offices and authorities were duly notified. Thus the stage was set for the "black" Sunday to follow.

Black Sunday–December 12, 1937

The U.S.S. *Panay* passed the night uneventfully. The crew and passengers kept watching the mounting flames in Nanking as Japanese artillerymen stepped up their fire. The American tankers had anchored as close to the gunboat as they could, and they too passed an uneventful night.

At 8:14 on Sunday morning, Japanese artillery suddenly began firing near the ships again, so Lieutenant Commander Hughes ordered his group under way. He set a course upriver to keep clear of the falling shells.

At about 9:40, after receiving a signal from a military unit ashore, the *Panay* stopped to receive a boarding party of a Japanese army lieutenant, a noncommissioned officer, and two heavily armed soldiers. Commander Hughes, coldly polite, answered those questions he felt obliged to answer. However, he stood on his neutrality rights in refusing to answer questions about Chinese soldiers or ships he had seen. For the same reason — and also because the *Panay* was a naval vessel and the tankers were under her convoy — Hughes refused the lieutenant's request to search any of the vessels.

After the boarding party left the ship, the *Panay* proceeded upriver for another hour and anchored in a section of the river known as the Hohsien Cutoff, about 27 miles above Nanking. Secretary Atcheson immediately fired off a message to the American consul-general in Shanghai, notifying him of the new position of the ship and requesting him to forward this information to the Japanese authorities. This was done.

At 1:35 in the afternoon, a lookout on the *Panay* spotted several

The Panay *on the fateful morning of December 12, 1937, starts up the Yangtze River to avoid shells falling on Nanking. (Charles Phelps Cushing)*

planes high overhead. They were approaching the anchorage from the southeast. When he received this report, Commander Hughes ran topside and tried to identify the planes with his 7X50 binoculars, but they were too high. Later investigation would reveal that there were twenty-four planes in all, but personnel on the *Panay* that day could not agree as to the number — actually they had little time to count.

Army Captain Roberts hurried topside when the word came

that planes had been sighted. Correspondents Alley, Marshall, Mac-
Donald, and James were already there. None of them could agree
as to the number, and no national markings were visible at this time.
Moreover, identification was doubly difficult because the planes were
approaching from out of the sun.

High overhead, squadron leader Shigeharu Murata, in command
of three Mitsubishi high-level bombers, designated the target below
and ordered the squadron to start its bombing run. They were flying
at approximately 11,000 feet.

Just behind and slightly above Murata's three planes, Lieutenant
Matsatake Okumiya's six dive bombers sighted the target and prepared to start their bombing dive. Lieutenant Komaki's six dive

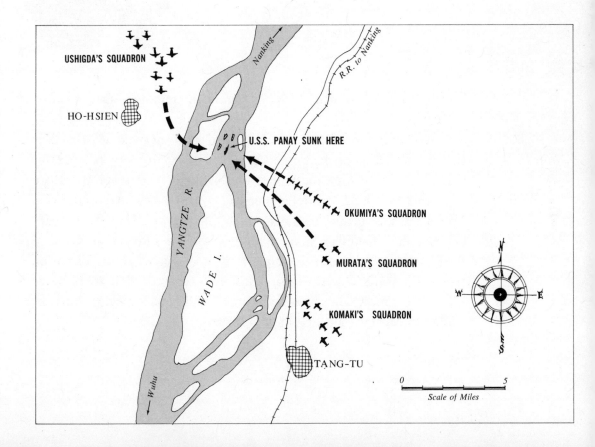

One of Lieutenant Okumiya's dive bombers makes its diving run on the Panay. *(U.S. Navy)*

bombers and Lieutenant Ushioda's nine fighters anxiously awaited their turn.

According to Lieutenant Okumiya, who survived World War II, the Japanese pilots had no inkling that their targets were not Chinese ships evacuating soldiers from Nanking, and were therefore legitimate targets. The intelligence had come to Rear Admiral Teizo Mitsunami's air group headquarters at Changchow from Lieutenant Commander Takeshi Aoki, who was liaison officer on General Asaka's staff. Army staff headquarters had received the information from an advanced army unit. This unit reported that there were seven large merchant ships and three smaller ones fleeing upriver, loaded to capacity with Chinese soldiers.

[24]

Murata's bombers each dropped six 60-kilogram bombs. Okumiya's dive bombers released both 250- and 60-kilogram bombs — not all of his planes carried the same type of bomb — at 500 meters. Komaki's squadron of dive bombers released 60-kilogram bombs at about the same height and then Lieutenant Ushioda's fighters swooped down for some low-level strafing.

Chief Quartermaster J. H. Lang, who was on the bridge with Commander Hughes, sighted the bombs first. Shouting a warning, he and Hughes ducked into the pilothouse. Just below them Captain Roberts had raised his binoculars to make another attempt at identification.

At that moment all hell broke loose aboard the *Panay* as the first

Panay sailors run to general quarters as the first bombs hit. (Charles Phelps Cushing)

John H. Paxton, secretary of the American embassy in Nanking, suffered an arm wound aboard the Panay. *Photo was taken later in the day aboard a rescue ship. (United Press International)*

bomb hit the ship on the port side forward. Roberts was knocked flat by the explosion even though he was well aft. On the bridge, Commander Hughes was thrown against the engine order telegraph by the blast, his left leg broken and his face and head cut.

Ensign Biwerse, who was down on the main deck forward, was the closest man to the first hit on the *Panay*. The blast stripped him bare of his uniform, knocking him several yards aft where he sat in a dazed condition.

Even those men who were belowdecks felt the severe concussion of the explosion. Secretary Paxton, who was working with Gassie in the ship's office, was thrown completely across the small room. Gassie's leg was broken by slamming against a safe.

On the top deck Norman Alley and Norman Soong were busy photographing the entire attack. Their newsman's instincts had made them grab their cameras almost before the shock of the first blast had worn off.

Those who had been knocked off their feet by the first high-level bombs were flattened again as the dive bombers scored hits on the *Panay*. Many had tried to take cover but were caught in the open. Okumiya's dive bombers scored near-misses with explosions close enough to the ship to rock it and lay low anyone exposed on deck. Shell fragments pockmarked the side of the gunboat.

Before Komaki's planes began their dives, the Americans had time to man the pitifully inadequate 30-caliber machine guns. By this time, shock had given way to towering rage on the part of the sailors, who turned the air blue with curses. The wounded were hurried below and those not actually manning guns took cover in the sick bay, in the chief petty officers' quarters, and in the engine room.

On the top deck, Norman Alley, Norman Soong, and Eric Mayell were very busy indeed. Taking newsreel pictures when they were able, ducking and hiding when bombs and machine-gun fire drove them to cover, they had little time to think about the danger. When they did, it was to realize that they might be photographing one of naval history's most dramatic moments. But at the time none of them realized the damning evidence they were piling up for the United States against the Japanese government.

When Komaki's dive bombers roared in for the attack, they scored several hits and left more people wounded aboard the *Panay*. The Italian newspaperman Sandro Sandri received his fatal wounds from either fragments or bullets during this attack. A veteran of the Ethiopian Campaign, he had seen men die before. When he felt his left side over the ribs and realized how badly he had been hit, he knew he would not live. Army Captain Roberts and others in the sick bay with Sandri were also peppered with steel fragments and

Top photo shows a gaping hole in the Panay's deck from one of the first bomb hits. Bottom, Panay begins to list, her sides pocked by shrapnel. (United Press International; Charles Phelps Cushing)

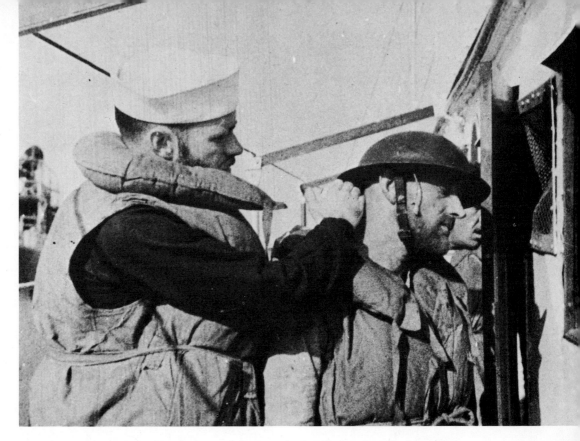

A sailor bandages a shipmate's wound during the height of the attack on the Panay. *(Charles Phelps Cushing)*

their clothes were torn, but none of the others were severely wounded.

The executive officer, Lieutenant Anders, although badly wounded on both hands, tried to man a machine gun himself. Unable to get it working, he headed for the pilothouse. While he and the quartermaster on watch were attempting to get the badly wounded Hughes below, Anders was splattered with bomb fragments. Shrapnel slashed his throat and rendered him unable to talk. When the wounded Commander Hughes gave him orders, the speechless executive officer wrote them on the bulkheads or on scraps of paper for Lieutenant Geist, who was also wounded, to pass on to the appropriate men.

Lieutenant Clark G. Grazier of the Navy Medical Corps was a man much in demand. Fortunately he escaped injury when the first devastating blast rocked the ship, although he was topside at the time. He quickly set up a sick bay in the upper level of the boiler room and went to work. There was plenty to do, even though some of the wounded refused treatment if they could walk. They had but one thought in mind — man the guns and destroy a Japanese plane. Chief Quartermaster Lang, wounded in several places and bleeding profusely, refused medical attention while he fired a machine gun at the attacking aircraft.

"Abandon Ship!"

At 2:05 P.M., with the *Panay* settling in the water and listing, Commander Hughes gave the order to abandon ship. At this time there were some 5 or 6 feet of water in the ship and there was no power available, either for propelling the vessel or for running the pumps. Only the captain's launch and a 22-foot sampan equipped with an outboard motor were available to evacuate the crew and passengers. Obviously other means of flotation were necessary, so overboard went mattresses, wooden doors, and anything else that could keep a man afloat. There were life jackets for all but a few, and several sailors removed theirs so that each of the civilians could have one.

Thanks to the experienced chief petty officers on board, the abandon ship operation went smoothly. Although wounded, Chief Lang herded the civilians toward the small boats, and Chief Ernest ("Swede") Mahlmann was everywhere, doing everything. When the first bomb had exploded he was just getting dressed. He immediately started manning a machine gun wearing only his shirt and undershorts. Norman Alley's photo of the trouserless gunner made headlines in many papers back in the States.

Lieutenant Anders sent the wounded Commander Hughes ashore in the first boat and quickly loaded the second. On the way toward shore, Japanese planes swooped low, machine guns chattered, and Machinist's Mate Second Class Kozak was wounded as bullets stitched a path across the boat.

Meanwhile, the three Standard Oil tankers in the convoy were having their troubles. The *Meian* took a bad hit and drifted downriver out of control where she grounded on the north shore. The

[31]

Crew begins to abandon ship shortly after 2:00 P.M. Note sailor removing his shoes before jumping into water below. (U.S. Navy)

Meiping, also badly hit, headed for a pontoon dock located on the south bank. Some one hundred Japanese soldiers appeared and ordered the crew and civilian passengers ashore. They gave the wounded civilians first-aid treatment. The tanker *Meihsia* closed toward the *Panay* in an effort to help. She was virtually untouched and her skipper, Captain Mender, wanted to be of assistance.

The crew of the *Panay*, frantic at the thought that the tanker with its thousands of gallons of gasoline was tied up alongside during a bombing attack, waved her off. However, she closed to within 2

This is Norman Alley's famous photo of Chief Ernest ("Swede") Mahlmann manning a machine gun aboard the Panay — *minus his trousers. It made the front page of many papers back in the States. (U.S. Navy)*

Boats from the Panay *bringing survivors ashore under fire of Japanese planes.* *(Charles Phelps Cushing)*

feet of the gunboat's bow and Jim Marshall, having heard the order to abandon ship, abandoned the *Panay* by leaping onto the *Meihsia's* deck.

The *Panay's* two boats with their second load shoved off as soon as they could be filled. Lieutenant Anders, who was barely able to stay on his feet, refused to go. Second Secretary George Atcheson also refused to leave until Army Captain Roberts threatened to throw him bodily into the boat.

After what seemed an eternity, the two boats returned a third time and evacuated all those who were still on board. The wounded and speechless Anders had to be helped into the boat by this time. One of Anders' last commands concerning the *Panay*, written on a bloodstained chart, was to check on the confidential publications aboard so they would not fall into Japanese hands. Ensign Biwerse had already tossed overboard those publications that he had weighted down for just such an emergency. But he could not manage to open the jammed communications safe to destroy other codes. In any case, they were soon to sink with the ship.

Survivors landing on the east side of the Yangtze River. (U.S. Navy)

Last moments of the U.S.S. Panay, *with her decks awash. (Charles Phelps Cushing)*

Lieutenant Geist made a valiant effort to salvage some forty thousand dollars that was in the ship's safe, but it, too, had been jammed shut by the explosions and Geist could not force it open.

At 3:05 P.M., the last man off the *Panay*, Ensign Biwerse, jumped into the rescue boat. Both of these small craft then steered for shore as the *Panay* settled slowly in the water, her colors still flying. Yet she still remained afloat!

If the *Meiping* personnel on the south shore thought they were safe from more bombing with so many Japanese soldiers around, they

Four correspondents who escaped from the sinking Panay *on this sampan were (from left) Weldon James (wearing flat cap) of United Press; Norman Soong of the* New York Times; *Colin MacDonald of the London* Times; *and Luigi Barzini, an Italian writer. (United Press International)*

were completely mistaken. True, there had been a fire on the ship, but the eight *Panay* sailors who had gone aboard for recreation prior to the bombing managed to put the fire out. The tanker *Meihsia* had moored alongside the *Meiping*, and to the Japanese pilots, these nested tankers presented a beautiful target. Two Japanese soldiers took up a position on the pontoon and started waving Japanese flags. But the attacking pilots paid as little attention to their own flags as they had to the Stars and Stripes. When the bombs started to fall, all hands on both ships ran for shore along the pontoon dock, but not before the Standard Oil personnel and American sailors tried to evacuate all the wounded. Correspondent Jim Marshall took a nasty fragment cut in the neck during this attack.

The *Panay*'s small boats completed their third trip ashore and Anders' first concern was to get the wounded under cover among the 10-foot-tall reeds covering the swampy Yangtze River bank. It was a particularly trying time for these wounded men. The ground was half-frozen and in places it was a sticky, slippery mess that was difficult to walk on. Clambering up the riverbank was back-breaking even for those who were still able-bodied. As for the wounded, they had to suffer through all the slipping, sliding efforts of their shipmates who were trying their hardest to be gentle with them.

It rapidly became apparent that more supplies were seriously needed. The *Panay*, while settling lower now in the water, was still

Pictured here is Chief Quartermaster John H. Lang, who was wounded when the first bomb struck the Panay. *Lang and other crew members scan the skies for attacking Japanese planes as they take cover among the tall reeds along the Yangtze. (U.S. Navy)*

afloat. Chief Petty Officer Mahlmann, along with Machinist's Mate Weimer, volunteered to return to the ship for such gear as they might salvage. They made the trip to the ship safely, but on their return two Japanese patrol boats appeared. Either they did not see or they ignored the boat from the *Panay*, because after machine-gunning the American gunboat they put several soldiers aboard the sinking *Panay*. The soldiers stayed but a few minutes, after which the Japanese patrol boats picked them up and departed upriver.

If the Americans had any doubts about mistaken identity, they were dispelled by this shooting incident, for the *Panay*'s flags were still flying!

As if to confirm the survivors' suspicions three bombers made an appearance overhead and one of them commenced to circle the marsh area. Secretary George Atcheson commented later that "the actions of this plane and the previous action of the Japanese army patrol boats, in connection with the incredible fact of the bombing of the *Panay*, gave us every reason to believe the Japanese were searching for us to destroy the witnesses to the bombing." There were no doubters left among the survivors.

At 3:54 P.M. the *Panay* sank. The party ashore now needed to get out of the area and obtain help. Of the *Panay*'s officers, Hughes, Anders, and Geist were wounded and Biwerse still suffered from the shock of the near-miss at the onset of the bombing. Dr. Grazier had more than enough to do. Army Captain Roberts, with the concurrence of Commander Hughes, assumed the leadership of the group.

Roberts decided to send Paxton off for help and to try to get word of the crew's plight to the American authorities. First, however, he sent Yuan Te-erk, a mess attendant originally from Shanghai, inland to reconnoiter. Yuan returned with the information that a walled town called Hoshien lay some 8 miles upriver. Paxton, with

The end of the Panay. *Murky waters of the Yangtze close over the American gunboat only moments before the Japanese made their final attack — despite American flags displayed on the ship's superstructure and flying from her masts.* (*United Press International*)

Andrew Wisler, the *Panay*'s communications expert, and Far Z. Wong, another mess attendant, then headed for Hoshien to get help and to make arrangements for receiving the survivors.

After a hard night of traveling, the entire party reached Hoshien half-frozen, hungry, and dead-tired. It was discovered that the

[41]

Commander Hughes, Panay's skipper, grins gamely as he lies in the reeds on the shores of the Yangtze, badly wounded. (Charles Phelps Cushing)

local magistrate was a graduate of Syracuse University in New York State. This was the last thing Captain Roberts expected to find in a tiny walled village in the heart of China, and the local authority proved a godsend to the worried leader. Although Japanese planes still ominously circled the area, the Chinese helped the Americans in every way they could. The party was saddened that night by the deaths of Sandri and Charles Ensminger, a petty officer.

The following morning, December 13, George Atcheson

reached an American missionary doctor in the town of Anking, and another at Luchowfu, both of whom relayed his message to Ambassador Nelson Johnson in Hankow. Help was soon on the way.

On the other side of the Yangtze River, the eight *Panay* crewmen and Jim Marshall, refugees from the now destroyed tankers, had better luck. Marshall and a seaman named Hodges started for Wuhu, the nearest large town. They were picked up by the Japanese and returned to Shanghai by plane. The other seven men headed inland and were rescued by an armed search party from the British gunboat H.M.S. *Bee.*

Panay crew members look on helplessly as the Italian journalist Sandro Sandri lies mortally wounded among the reeds on the shores of the Yangtze River. (U.S. Navy)

An outstanding hero of the Panay *incident was the executive officer, Lieutenant Arthur Anders. The wounded officer lies on a stretcher on the banks of the Yangtze as Chief Boatswain's Mate E. R. Uhlman, also wounded, examines the lieutenant. (United Press International)*

Another wounded officer of the Panay was Lieutenant J. W. Geist, whose leg was hit by shrapnel as the Japanese bombed the gunboat. He is pictured here aboard the rescue ship. (United Press International)

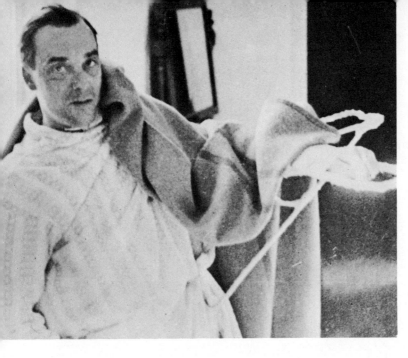

Wounded newsman Jim Marshall is shown here recuperating in a naval hospital after the Panay incident. (United Press International)

A group of Panay survivors resting at Hanshan, en route to Shanghai. (United Press International)

As It Looked from Shanghai

On board the cruiser U.S.S. *Augusta*, flagship of the Asiatic Fleet, Admiral Yarnell had been in constant radio communication with Ambassador Nelson T. Johnson in Hankow. Johnson used the U.S.S. *Luzon*'s radio room as a link with Shanghai, Peking, Tokyo, and Washington. The U.S.S. *Oahu* was in Kiukiang, some 200 miles upriver relaying messages when needed. Atcheson was, of course, using the *Panay*'s radio room to clear his traffic. The flow of radio traffic, both routine and of a more urgent nature, was constant, with the three gunboats almost always in touch with one another.

On December 12, at 1:35 P.M., during a transmission to the *Luzon* from the *Panay*, the latter abruptly ceased transmitting in the middle of a dispatch. The *Luzon* radio watch logged it as "incomplete" and thought no more of it. Admiral Yarnell, however, began to get anxious when three hours passed with no word from the *Panay*. He was well aware of her dangerous position. In the next transmission to the *Luzon* he asked the commander of the Yangtze Patrol, Rear Admiral Marquart, to investigate.

Neither the *Luzon*, the *Oahu*, nor any of the British gunboats could raise the *Panay* on the radio, but Yarnell did receive the disturbing news in a dispatch from the commander of the Yangtze Patrol that the *Luzon* had received word of Japanese army intentions to fire on all vessels in the river, regardless of nationality.

The situation became even more serious when Admiral Yarnell was informed that the H.M.S. *Ladybird* and the H.M.S. *Bee* had been shelled by Japanese army units above Nanking. The *Ladybird* received six or seven hits and one man was killed and four were

The cruiser U.S.S. Augusta, *flagship of the Asiatic Fleet. (U.S. Navy)*

From left, U.S.S. Oahu, *H.M.S.* Bee, *and H.M.S.* Ladybird *waiting in the Yangtze River to rescue survivors from the* Panay. *(U.S. Navy)*

wounded. Nearer Nanking the H.M.S. *Cricket* and the H.M.S. *Scarab* were dive-bombed.

It was not until the next morning that Admiral Yarnell received a message from Admiral Marquart confirming the loss of the *Panay*. The message furnished few details but it did state that Secretary Atcheson was safe and that Commander Hughes had a broken leg.

Not far away from the *Augusta*, Vice Admiral Kiyoshi Hasegawa, the supreme Japanese naval commander in China aboard the cruiser *Idzumo*, knew more than Yarnell about the event. He had learned of the disaster the night before, and on Monday morning the squadron commanders who had attacked the *Panay* were aboard with explanations for the admiral and his assembled staff.

Hasegawa was particularly annoyed because the attacks were in complete disregard of his orders not to attack shipping in the river without positive identification. The admiral was aware of the fact that little or no Chinese shipping remained afloat and that any ships sighted were virtually certain to be neutral. He was also suspicious of the army leaders; there was no love lost between the Japanese army and navy. Only the year before, the esteemed and aged Admiral Viscount Saito, a graduate of the U.S. Naval Academy, was assassinated by a radical group of young army officers from the Tokyo garrison. Admiral Suzuki was gravely wounded in the same affair. Hasegawa was well aware of the strength of the intensely nationalistic army groups within the command and considered them barbaric in their conduct toward foreign military officers. His first thought was to send an officer to Admiral Yarnell.

Lieutenant Okumiya, standing by after his interview, said: "But we again felt the gravity of our unfortunate error upon seeing Rear Admiral Rokuzo Sugiyema, the Chief of Staff, grave visaged and

[49]

sorrowful, as he departed to tender apologies to Admiral Yarnell for our action."

Admiral Hasegawa gave immediate orders to load doctors and medical supplies aboard two flying boats and proceed to the scene. Medical supplies and a team of doctors also left Changchow Airfield at his orders almost at the same time to supplement the Shanghai group. Then the admiral left the *Idzumo* to proceed to the *Augusta* in order to tender his personal regrets for the "unfortunate affair of mistaken identity." Hasegawa knew that even though he was not directly responsible, the ultimate responsibility was his as commander in chief. To his credit, he was ready to accept full responsibility and requested his own recall.

By Monday afternoon Admiral Yarnell was furious when the Japanese began this round of apologies. He received Hasegawa coldly, yet politely. But the Japanese were well aware of Yarnell's seething rage. As new reports filtered in, it became apparent to all on the flagship that the attack might well have been deliberate.

The Reaction in Tokyo

"December 13, 1937

This was a black day indeed."

So began the diary of the American ambassador to Japan, Joseph C. Grew, on the day he learned of the *Panay*'s sinking. That very morning, before he had actually received news of the sinking, the ambassador had called on the Japanese minister of foreign affairs, Koki Hirota, because alarming reports of indiscriminate shelling in and around Nanking had reached him by telegram during the night. Grew warned Hirota that he had received reports that the Japanese army had ordered their artillery to fire on all ships without regard for nationality. The American ambassador reminded the Japanese foreign minister of his earlier warning in September: namely, that although Americans were pacific and patient people, the lessons of history must not be forgotten and that the Spanish-American War slogan "Remember the *Maine!*" had been one of those painful lessons.

About four hours after this meeting, when Hirota called at the American embassy, he was probably remembering his American history. He had just learned of the *Panay*'s sinking and had immediately proceeded to Grew's office to express "the profound apologies and regrets" of the Japanese government. On his own he added something beyond the usual formal diplomatic expressions: "I can't tell you how badly we feel about all this."

The minister of the navy, Admiral Yonai, and the minister of war, General Nakamura, lost no time in adding their regrets to those of the foreign minister.

Ambassador Grew fired off a priority cable to Washington with a short summary of Hirota's call and regrets. It crossed a similar high-

[51]

American Ambassador and Mrs. Joseph C. Grew at the American embassy in Tokyo. (Charles Phelps Cushing)

priority dispatch from the State Department reporting their information as received from Ambassador Johnson in Hankow. This dispatch directed Grew to gather all the information he could from Japanese sources, to request the Japanese to take appropriate action to prevent any more such incidents, and lastly to impress on Hirota the gravity of the situation.

Hirota needed no prodding to understand the severity of the situation. Indeed, by this time he knew how Grew felt and realized that it represented the reaction he could expect from America.

At the U.S. embassy, American representatives of the Associated Press, United Press, and the New York *Herald Tribune* bombarded the ambassador with questions. Yet Grew could tell them little more than they had already learned from Japanese sources. Expressions of regret and sympathy for the families of the *Panay* dead and wounded poured into the embassy from Japanese people in all walks of life. Schoolchildren, professional men, officials, and educators tried to impress upon the ambassador their shame at the tragic event.

The common people and even those officials highly placed in the Japanese government did not at this time realize the seriousness of the incident. Not until four days later did the reports of the machine-gunning of the sinking *Panay* by army launches, and the strafing of the survivors by airplane, reach Tokyo. Ambassador Grew commented: "These statements added to others presented to the Shanghai Court of Inquiry made the incident appear very much worse than we had first thought."

The vice minister of the navy, Admiral Yamamoto, with several of his staff and two investigating officers newly returned from Shanghai called on Ambassador Grew to present him with certain facts concerning the incident. Ambassador Grew set the vice minister straight by stating the United States government's position. Briefly it was this:

1. U.S. ships were on the river by right.
2. Their approximate position was known to Japanese military authorities.
3. The ships were clearly marked with American flags.
4. The ships were bombed by Japanese naval planes at low altitude and the *Panay* was machine-gunned and boarded after the Americans abandoned her.
5. The survivors were machine-gunned by Japanese planes.

This was a damning condemnation of the Japanese military

[53]

*Japanese Admiral Yama-
moto. (Charles Phelps
Cushing)*

establishment and Yamamoto realized it. Ambassador Grew went on
to state that he would have no more to say until the findings of the
American Court of Inquiry, then in session on the U.S.S. *Augusta*,
were complete. While the ambassador was impressed by the admiral's
frankness and desire to set the record straight, he did lose his temper
momentarily with the army representative, Colonel Shibayama, when
the latter suggested that perhaps the survivors' reports might be in-
coherent.

The Reaction in Washington

When word of the *Panay* sinking reached Franklin D. Roosevelt, the American president, he reacted immediately. Sending a curt memorandum to Secretary of State Cordell Hull, he directed that cabinet officer to tell the Japanese ambassador that "the President is deeply shocked and concerned by the news of indiscriminate bombing of American and other non-Chinese vessels on the Yangtze and that he requests that the Emperor be so advised." The word "requests" was written in the president's hand in place of "suggests" which appeared in the original draft.

The memorandum further asked for a full apology, compensation, and guarantees against a repetition of such attacks. Roosevelt well knew he was making it extremely difficult for the Japanese government. To the Japanese mind, Emperor Hirohito was regarded as a divinity, and was thus aloof from governmental problems. The president knew he presented Foreign Minister Hirota with a doubly difficult problem: first, how to bring it to the emperor's attention; second, how to avoid bringing it to his attention without offending the United States.

Congress also reacted immediately — and in a strange manner. The Ludlow proposal, introduced by Congressman Louis Ludlow of Indiana, sought to amend the United States Constitution to make it illegal for Congress to declare war except in the case of armed invasion. In all other cases, Ludlow wanted a nationwide referendum. Moreover, the congressman had 200 signatures on a petition to get his bill out of committee and onto the House floor. The *Panay* incident prompted enough additional signatures from other congressmen to reach the necessary majority of 218.

[55]

New York Times.

Copyright, 1937, by The New York Times Company.

LATE CITY EDITION
Generally fair and continued cold today. Tomorrow mostly cloudy, probably snow, slightly warmer.
Temperatures Yesterday—Max., 28; Min., 19

NEW YORK, TUESDAY, DECEMBER 14, 1937.

PP   TWO CENTS In New York City.   THREE CENTS Within 200 Miles. | FOUR CENTS Elsewhere Except In 7th and 8th Postal Zones.

U. S. DEMANDS FULL SATISFACTION FROM JAPAN, WITH GUARANTEE AGAINST FURTHER ATTACKS; THOUGHT SHIPS CHINESE, ADMIRAL EXPLAINS

AKEN UP 282-123; IS BITTER

s North in Futile Fight nmittal

SSAILS FOES

get for False ys—Defends Clause

YORK TIMES.
Dec. 13.—Before he House today he second item special-session es and Hours

the Black-Con-the Senate late w having more nts attached in mmittee.
iittee] reported an 18-to-2 vote ained, buried in committee until harge petition 123.

rt of the meas-Mary Norton, or Committee. wenty minutes ebate on Mrs. discharge the m further con-and four hours general debate. extended the x hours. es of Texas, on to the mo-e Rules Com-he bill as re-Committee was ored by those discharge pe-ly changed by

pposition bill that labor shouted. "You business, small

a measure was labor, that it t it would not ries and then It should be dustries from

NANKING OCCUPIED, JAPANESE REPORT

They Announce Fall of the City After Bitter All-Day Battle —Chinese Dispute Claim

SHIPS SHELL DEFENDERS

Invaders Hint They Will Push Into Heart of China—New Regime Set Up at Peiping

Special Cable to THE NEW YORK TIMES.
SHANGHAI, Tuesday, Dec. 14.—The Japanese Army headquarters here announced last night that Japanese troops had completed the occupation of Nanking. It was just a few hours less than four months after hostilities had begun on the outskirts of Shanghai.
It was announced that the occu-

Windsor Castle to Have Shelters From Bombing

Special Cable to THE NEW YORK TIMES.
LONDON, Dec. 13.—Scores of underground passages in Windsor Castle, where the royal family spends more time than anywhere else except Buckingham Palace, are to be converted into bomb-proof and gas-proof shelters. The decision symbolizes the compre-hensiveness of precautions that the government is now taking for the British people after years of inaction resulting from a dispute with local authorities over the division of costs.
It also shows how much more the dangers of a bombing attack are appreciated than during the World War. The Buckingham Palace roof then was protected with a netting and sandbags. These were never tested, but ex-perts say they would be virtually useless against a present-day bomb.

JAPANESE WORRIED

See Blow to Their Hope of Driving America and Britain Apart

RESCUE WORK CONTINUES

British Gunboat Presses Hunt for Survivors of Panay and Three Oil Vessels

By HALLETT ABEND
Wireless to THE NEW YORK TIMES.
SHANGHAI, Tuesday, Dec. 14.—Japanese officials here are hourly becoming more appalled over the attacks on the United States gun-boat Panay and the British gun-boats Ladybird, Bee, Cricket and Scarab and a dozen unarmed Amer-ican and British river steamers.
The main Japanese hope was to win America away from her pres-ent cordiality with Britain and to do all possible to overcome the anti-Japanism prevalent among the American public, but responsible leaders now realise that the blun-ders of irresponsible Japanese fliers and shore commanders are further alienating the American public and officialdom.
The United States flagship Au-gusta, which had been scheduled to sail from Shanghai today carrying Admiral Harry E. Yarnell to Ma-nila, will remain here indefinitely, as will the cruiser Marblehead, which has just arrived, intending to re[i]eve the Augusta.

Japanese Boast Cited
It was understood that the atti-tude of the United States Navy would be that this Japanese cam-paign of attacking foreign gunboats was utterly indefensible because the Japanese had been boasting that they had sunk every Chinese gun-boat on the Yangtze River.
At noon yesterday the utmost ten-sion prevailed aboard the Augusta, where Admiral Yarnell anchored

THE WHITE HOUSE
WASHINGTON

Memorandum handed to the Secretary of State at 12:30 P. M., December 13, 1937.

Please tell the Japanese Ambassador when you see him at one o'clock:

1. That the President is deeply shocked and concerned by the news of indis-criminate bombing of American and other non-Chinese vessels on the Yangtze, and that he suggests that the Emperor be so advised.

2. That all the facts are being assembled and will shortly be presented to the Japanese Government.

3. That in the meantime it is hoped the Japanese Government will be considering definitely for presentation to this Government:
   a. Full expressions of re-gret and proffer of full compensation;
   b. Methods guaranteeing against a repetition of any similar attack in the future.

F.R.

Wired Photo—Times Wide World
PRESIDENT'S MEMORANDUM ON THE PANAY

GUNBOAT ATTACKS AROUSE BRITISH IRE

'Strong' Protest Is Made In Tokyo—Eden Confers With United States Charge

CONGRESS OPINION SHARPLY DIVIDED

Some Members Demand Recall of Troops and Ships, Others Insist on a Firm Course

PLEA TO EMPEROR

Roosevelt Requests That His Grave Feeling Be Told to Hirohito

NO ACTION IS INDICATED

United States and Britain Are Driven to Closer Unity by Yangtze Attacks

Special to THE NEW YORK TIMES.
WASHINGTON, Dec. 13.—Presi-dent Roosevelt moved swiftly today to meet the grave situation pre-sented by the sinking of the United States gunboat Panay above Nan-king by Japanese naval aviators. Full expressions of regret and full compensation were demanded of Japan as well as guarantees against a repetition of any similar attack in the future.
The demands were made on the the President's behalf by Secretary of State Cordell Hull to Hirosi Saito, the Japanese Ambassador. They carried with them a request that Emperor Hirohito be advised how deeply shocked and concerned the President was over the indis-criminate bombing of American and other non-Chinese vessels on the Yangtze.
The fact that Mr. Roosevelt di-rected that his feelings be conveyed directly to the Emperor emphasized the gravity with which he viewed the situation, notwithstanding the fact that Japan had already ac-cepted full responsibility and had apologized both here and in Tokyo to this government.
The protest, which was delivered by Secretary Hull to Ambassador Saito at the State Department this noon, will be supplemented by a strong note of protest following the lines of the oral statements made today but setting forth the position

---

Front-page headlines such as this one in the United States reflected American indignation concerning the Panay incident.

This serious consideration of the Ludlow amendment gave the Japanese consolation in knowing that America was not about to go to war over the sinking. However, Roosevelt's demanding note and the temper of a great part of the country, particularly when the entire story was known and pictures of the incident were seen, left no doubt in Japanese minds that a mandate for war could soon be whipped up by a determined administration. Actually, powerful interests were backing the president in this attempt to take the direction of foreign policy out of his hands. For example, Arthur Krock of the *New York Times* called the amendment "dream-born" and a "museum piece."

Alf Landon, the Republican candidate who opposed Roosevelt in the 1936 election, sent an immediate note of support to the president when he heard of the Ludlow resolution's progress. Earlier he had agreed to support the Democrats in foreign affairs. He reiterated his support for the administration's handling of the affair, and denounced congressmen who would "hamstring your conduct of extremely delicate foreign situations."

Yet despite the tense atmosphere prevailing in the capital, the annual White House Reception for the Diplomatic Corps took place on schedule, just four days after the sinking. Ambassador Saito of Japan and Ambassador Wang of China made sure to be there. It was the high point of the social season.

Time magazine reported that "the U.S. is in a salutary mood of reasonableness in dealing with Japan. And Secretary Hull, counseled on all sides not to act hastily, was in the strange position of a lawyer whose client had been injured, being pressed not to sue for damages."

Although the United States had sent the sharpest diplomatic note to a foreign power since World War I, the general reaction

[57]

throughout the country was the hope that the nation would not become involved in a war.

The State Department, concerned over what it considered a conspicuous delay in an answer to Roosevelt's note, finally received a full and satisfying answer to that note on Christmas Day. This note arrived shortly before the findings of the Court of Inquiry were received, and both the apology and findings were published simultaneously in the United States.

Secretary of State Hull dryly reminded the Japanese government that the United States would rely on the findings of the Court of Inquiry of the United States Navy rather than on the Japanese findings for the "origins, causes, and circumstances" of the incident.

How It Looked to the World

Within the United States, the press, alerted by early rumors from the State Department and the White House, desperately tried to find out what had happened in China. Its Shanghai representatives knew only what the American consulate told them. For the moment, Admiral Yarnell and his staff were quiet. In Tokyo, United Press, Associated Press, and individual newspaper correspondents got the word from the American embassy — first, the incomplete report to the ambassador from Foreign Minister Hirota, and second, the terse dispatch sent by Rear Admiral Marquart of YangPat on December 13 at 10:03 A.M. This message stated only that the *Panay* was sunk, that Secretary Atcheson was safe, and that Commander Hughes had suffered a broken leg. This was enough for the papers to carry "U.S. Warship Sunk" headlines and to speculate on the details.

British papers carried the story prominently, suggesting that the United States might make a naval display in the Far East to bolster her strength there. The London press also speculated that Britain herself would send warships. The average Briton favored a solid front presented by Great Britain and the United States in order to forestall Japanese imperialistic designs on China. They had forgotten that the United States had suggested such a front several years earlier and they (the British) had backed off.

In Germany, National Air Minister Hermann Goering's *National Zeitung* warned Britain and the United States to remain neutral in the Sino-Japanese War. Benito Mussolini, following the lead of his German ally, declared that the Americans deserved the incident just for being where they were.

Strangely enough, this same view was shared by extreme paci-

Funeral cortege of the gunboat Panay *as seen from her sister ship, U.S.S. Oahu. Procession steams down the Yangtze toward Shanghai after pickup of survivors at the scene of the attack.*

fist groups within the United States, who wanted the country to go completely isolationist and let the rest of the world, including both Europe and the Far East, go ahead and slaughter each other. In Kansas—reflecting the opinion of some Midwest editors—the *Concordia Press* asked in an editorial, "What were Standard Oil tankers doing up the Yangtze River in the midst of a war zone? And why is it necessary to have U.S. war vessels plying up and down that river in the heart of China?"

In Kansas one could also find the opposite end of the spectrum of public opinion as reflected by the Oklahoma *Independent*. "This country is pacific and adverse to war, but it is not a set of abject cowards. . . . Our Pacific Fleet should long ago have been anchored off the Japan coast."

Bluejackets carry casket of Panay *victim aboard U.S.S.* Augusta *at Shanghai for shipment home. (United Press International)*

It might be added that the editor of this paper was the father of Army Captain Frank Roberts. The captain, at the moment of this publication, was arriving back at Shanghai, having led the survivors of the *Panay* to final safety aboard the *Augusta*.

Meanwhile, newsmen covering the bloody events in China were having a difficult time. Pembroke Stephens of the London *Telegraph* had been killed earlier in the fighting around Shanghai, and Hallet Abend and A. J. Billingham had been wounded. A. T. Steele of the Chicago *Daily News* and Menken's photo coverage of the "Rape of Nanking" were on their way to the States.

In Shanghai, Abend of the *New York Times* broke the story of Colonel Kingoro Hashimoto, the army commander in the Wuhu area, reportedly the officer who ordered his units to fire on all ships in the river.

As details of the machine-gunning of the *Panay* and the adventures of the survivors became known in the States, atrocity stories of the Japanese army occupation in Nanking also flooded the front pages of American newspapers. Correspondents who witnessed the hundreds of executions claimed that Japanese soldiers invited Japanese sailors to witness the massacre, and that they thoroughly enjoyed it. They further claimed that the soldiers were out of control of their officers, and for several days were engaged in raping, looting, and pillaging.

After reading these highly descriptive stories, Americans could no longer doubt the authenticity of the survivors' accounts of the *Panay* incident. They could not be dismissed as greatly exaggerated reports by shell-shocked survivors, as one Japanese officer tried to make the American authorities believe.

Visual Evidence

Admiral Harry Yarnell was itching to see the newsreel films that Norman Alley and Eric Mayell had taken — and had so carefully guarded — during their trek from the riverbank and return to the rescue gunboat, U.S.S. *Oahu*. These films were locked in the paymaster's safe under heavy marine guard. Yarnell also knew such evidence should reach the hands of the nation's highest authority at the earliest possible moment. He took immediate action to see that the films were taken to the States.

The day after the *Panay*'s survivors returned to the *Augusta*, four American destroyers left Shanghai early in the morning. Alley and the film were aboard the last destroyer, the U.S.S. *Stewart*.

Then began a trip halfway around the world. For the year 1937, it was accomplished in record time. The *Stewart* poured on the steam for the 1,100-mile run to Manila. At Manila, Alley, the precious film under his arm, and accompanied by a heavily armed guard, boarded the four-engined Martin Flying Clipper for the flight to the United States.

The plane stopped for fuel at Guam, Wake, Midway, Honolulu, and San Francisco. At each stop, armed guards took the film into custody until the plane was ready to take off again. At San Francisco four state policemen surrounded Alley and stayed with him until the plane touched down at Newark Airport. Here, two New Jersey state police joined the guard. An armored car picked up the film to rush it to Fort Lee for processing.

It was not until the next afternoon that Alley saw the films for the first time — when they were run in a projection room at Universal headquarters. What he saw sobered him. He realized he probably had the scoop of the century, but more important he realized he had succeeded in providing the nation's highest authorities with absolute proof of the deliberateness of the Japanese attack.

These highest authorities saw the film the next day in Washington, D.C. Alley himself had carried them down to the capital on the midnight train. Among others, the secretary of the navy, the secretary of war, and Senator Key Pittman, chairman of the Foreign Relations Committee, sat dumbfounded as they watched the Japanese attack unfold.

The president of the United States requested Alley to remove some 30 feet of the film. These 30 feet showed planes so low that one could almost see the expressions on the pilots' faces. Roosevelt, acting for the nation, had, five days before, accepted the Japanese apology officially. Accordingly, it would never do to let the American public see how really damaging the evidence was; it would serve only to agitate the nation further. Yet even without the 30 feet the film was spectacular.

The Naval Court of Inquiry

Admiral Harry Yarnell's Naval Court of Inquiry had been working night and day to complete its work in order to provide the president and the State Department with an official background of facts upon which they could place credence. Ambassador Grew had more or less left the acceptance of Japanese protestations of "error," "confusion of the hour," and other excuses dangling until his government had had the time to thoroughly investigate the *Panay* sinking.

The court, working feverishly in Shanghai, was composed of four naval officers: Captain H. V. McKittrick, Commander M. L. Deyo, Lieutenant Commander A. C. J. Sabalot, and Lieutenant C. V. Whiting as judge advocate.

This court submitted thirty-six findings of facts to Admiral Yarnell, who approved them in toto and forwarded the proceedings to Secretary of the Navy Swanson. The most damning facts concerning the Japanese position included in the report were points 11 through 16:

(11) That at about thirteen thirty-eight, three large Japanese twin-motored planes in a vee formation were observed at a considerable height passing overhead downriver. At this time no other craft were in the near vicinity of the *Panay* and convoy and there was no reason to believe the ships were in a dangerous area.

(12) That without warning these three Japanese planes released several bombs, one or two of which struck on or

very close to the bow of the U.S.S. *Panay* and another which struck on or very close to the S.S. *Meiping*.

(13) That the bombs of the first attack did considerable damage to the U.S.S. *Panay*, disabling the forward three-inch gun, seriously injuring the Captain and others, wrecking the pilot house and sick bay, disabling the radio equipment, the steaming fireroom, so that all power was lost and causing leaks in the hull which resulted in the ship settling down by the head and listing to starboard, thereby contributing fundamentally to the sinking of the ship.

(14) That immediately thereafter a group of six single-engined planes attacked from ahead, diving singly and appearing to concentrate on the U.S.S. *Panay*; a total of about twenty bombs were dropped many striking close aboard and creating by fragments and concussions great damage to ship and personnel. These attacks lasted about twenty minutes during which time at least two of the planes attacked also with machine guns; one machine gun attack was directed against a ship's boat bearing wounded ashore causing several further wounds and piercing the boat with bullets.

(15) That during the entire attack the weather was clear with high visibility and little if any wind.

(16) That the planes participating in the attacks on the U.S.S. *Panay* and its convoy were unmistakably identified by their markings as being Japanese.

As if the establishment of these facts did not sufficiently pin down the responsibility and give the lie to "poor visibility" and other

[67]

Japanese excuses, Admiral Yarnell sent to Secretary Swanson the court's official findings as follows:

Dec. 23, 1937
10:50 A.M.

From: Commander in Chief Asiatic Fleet
To: The Secretary of the Navy

The following is the opinion of the Court of Inquiry ordered to investigate the bombing and sinking of the U.S.S. *Panay*. The opinion is approved.

1. That the U.S.S. *Panay* was engaged in carrying out the established policy of the United States of protecting American lives and property.

2. That the Japanese aviators should have been familiar with the characteristics and distinguishing markings of the *Panay* as the ship was present at Nanking during the Japanese aerial attacks on this city.

3. That, while the first bombers might not have been able on account of their altitude to identify the U.S.S. *Panay*, there was no excuse for attacking without properly identifying the target, especially as it was well known that neutral vessels were present in the Yangtze River.

4. That it was utterly inconceivable that the six light bombing planes coming within about six hundred feet of the ships and attacking for over a period of twenty minutes could not be aware of the identity of the ships they were attacking.

5. That the Japanese were wholly and solely responsible

[68]

for all losses which have occurred as the result of this attack.

6. That the deaths of C. L. Ensminger, Sk first, and E. W. C. Hulsebus, coxswain, occurred in line of duty and were not the result of their own misconduct.

7. That the injured and wounded members of the crew of the U.S.S. *Panay* received their wounds and injuries in the line of duty and were not the result of their own misconduct.

8. In considering the case as a whole and attending incidents that the court is of the opinion that no offenses have been committeed nor blame incurred by any member of the naval service involved.

Only the night before, Ambassador Grew had received the vice minister of the Japanese navy, Admiral Yamamoto, and others, in the embassy. The purpose of this visit was to inform the ambassador of the facts as reported by Japanese officers sent to Nanking to investigate the "unfortunate affair." Grew said, in a telegram to the secretary of state, "The conference at the Embassy lasted 3½ hours. ... The main effort of these officers was clearly to lay before me the evidence to prove their contention that the bombing and subsequent machine gunning of the *Panay* and other American ships and survivors were mistakes and unintentional."

It had been ten days after this communication that President Roosevelt had requested Norman Alley and Universal Newsreel to remove the 30 feet of damning film of the bombing.

[69]

The Culprit of the *Panay* Affair

The Imperial Japanese Navy, through its Third Fleet commander in chief, Vice Admiral Kiyoshi Hasegawa, attempted to explain the *Panay* "error" to Admiral Harry Yarnell in Shanghai. Back in Tokyo, Admiral Yamamoto, vice minister of the navy, made every effort to convince Ambassador Grew that the Japanese navy had in fact blundered, and that the attack had not been premeditated. Indeed, it was true that Admiral Hasegawa had made every effort through his orders and directives to prevent just such a "mistake" as the sinking of the *Panay*.

But what about the Japanese army's role in the *Panay* affair?

It was a well-known fact that advance units of Lieutenant General Asaka's command advancing on Nanking had ravaged the towns and countryside of central China. At that time, military discipline was at a low ebb and there were good reasons to suspect that the army commanders wished to conceal certain facts filtering back to the Japanese home islands from the Nanking front.

The target information involving the *Panay* came from an army unit of Prince Asaka's command. One regiment, assigned the task of taking Wuhu, was advancing upstream on both sides of the Yangtze River. Colonel Kingoro Hashimoto, commanding that regiment, was known to be an ardent Nationalist who hated all Westerners. It was at his express command that artillery units of his regiment opened fire on the H.M.S. *Ladybird* just prior to the attack on the *Panay*.

British Rear Admiral Holt stormed ashore to protest the shelling. At Hashimoto's headquarters, the colonel admitted a "mistake" in firing on British ships but countered that he had orders to fire on all shipping in the river. Admiral Holt reported that Colonel Hashi-

[70]

moto did not act sufficiently contrite and relayed the warning to higher American and British authorities.

It was from this field headquarters that the rumor of ships carrying Chinese soldiers upriver originated. It was also a unit of this same command that machine-gunned the *Panay* just prior to her sinking.

The origin of the target designation, then, lay with Colonel Hashimoto. It was received in army headquarters and relayed to the Changchow naval air base by Lieutenant Commander Takeshi Aoki, a naval aviator on the general's staff. Hashimoto did not report to his commanding general any machine-gunning incidents, or the shelling of the *Ladybird*.

Thus, as the investigation by Japanese military authorities continued, the finger of guilt always seemed to point to Hashimoto. Who was this Japanese army officer and why was he so motivated?

Colonel Kingoro Hashimoto, a professional military man, was an ardent supporter of the famed "Tanaka Memorial." This paper, allegedly written by Premier Tanaka in 1929, became what amounted to the *Mein Kampf* of Japan. It was a manifesto that stated in no uncertain terms that Japan's domination of the entire world was the aim of the military men of that regime — if not of the government itself. Beginning with the conquest of China, the military would then take Indochina, the Philippines, the Dutch East Indies, India, and so on, until the entire world was conquered by the forces of Nippon.

Hashimoto himself was no stranger to violence. As a young officer, in 1917, he had served as military attaché to the Japanese embassy in Moscow. Here he had had a firsthand view of revolution in its most violent form.

In 1936 he was a leader in the army revolt that resulted in the assassination of former Premier Admiral Saito, the wounding of

[71]

Kingoro Hashimoto.
(Wide World Photos)

Admiral Suzuki, and the murder and wounding of other high government officials.

Although Colonel Hashimoto was not punished for his involvement, he was discharged from the army. He immediately organized a fascist-type youth group and exhorted them to purge the country of liberals. In 1937 he was recalled to the army and sent to China. Undoubtedly his superiors thought this firebrand should be buried in China for the good of the nation. But even in China there was ample reason to suspect that he was the villain of the *Panay* affair, and that he actually planned the attack on the gunboat.

Hashimoto's strength lay in his political affiliations and as a sometime member of the Japanese Diet. Even the highest army authorities were reluctant to reprimand him for fear he might cause additional divisions in an army already divided on national policy and the army's role in it. Using his political position as a speaking forum, Hashimoto had gained an impressive following among ultranationalistic army officers.

As it turned out, justice did not catch up with Hashimoto until after World War II. Along with other Japanese officers he was brought to trial before the War Crimes Commission. He admitted being a member of the secret Black Dragon Society, and a longtime advocate of Japanese control of the Far East. Yet he did not shed any light on the *Panay* affair during or after his trial. Hashimoto was sentenced to life imprisonment but was released after ten years in prison.

Effects and Aftermath

In Washington, officials waited impatiently for an answer to the president's note of protest delivered by Ambassador Grew to Foreign Minister Hirota on the fourteenth of December.

Characteristically, and in keeping with the Japanese line of thought, the answer reached Washington on Christmas Eve. Grew himself called the timing a masterstroke. The Japanese were relying heavily on the Americans' "Peace on Earth, Good Will . . ." attitude so prevalent on Christmas Day.

In their note, the Japanese expressed their abject apologies, admitted responsibility for the incident, and offered to make amends. The United States promptly (at 5 P.M. Christmas Day) accepted the apologies of the Japanese government and considered their note "responsive," that is, acceptable. The Americans also expressed hope that the actions already taken as well as those to be put into effect would prevent similar unfortunate incidents in the future. Indemnities, which were decided at a later date, amounted to $2,214,007. This debt was promptly paid.

Sumner Welles, that seasoned diplomat, probably reflected the attitude of most Americans when he said:

> I have always felt that the President, who handled the entire incident personally, could, under the conditions which then existed, have shown neither greater wisdom nor greater determination. His message sent directly to the Japanese Emperor, was admirably couched. The Japanese disavowal and offer to pay full indemnity was complete and immediate. The prestige and dignity of this country were fully upheld.

[74]

He added that the country was not prepared for, nor would the public permit, a "bellicose action."

Thus President Roosevelt, with his uncanny knack for reading the public's mind, had made the best of a sorry affair. Doubtless he remembered what General Douglas MacArthur, when he was chief of staff, said of power diplomacy: "Armies and navies in being efficient give weight to the peaceful words of statesmen, but a feverish effort to create them once a crisis is imminent simply provokes an attack." Indeed, Theodore Roosevelt's earlier statement, "Speak softly but carry a big stick," was a paraphrase of this attitude.

Accordingly, Franklin Roosevelt intended to waste no time in preparing his nation for a war that seemed more and more imminent. He wrote Chairman Edward Tally of the House of Representatives in January, 1938, that since preliminary estimates for an increase in the naval plan of construction for 1939 were put forth, "world events have caused me growing concern. . . . The fact is that in the world as a whole many nations are not only continuing but are enlarging their armament programs." The president then told of his efforts to stop this trend, his failure to do so, and added that he might send supplements to the congressionally approved building program.

In his State of the Union message in January, 1938, President Roosevelt said, without actually referring to the *Panay* incident by name, "I am thankful that I can tell you that our nation is at peace. It has been kept at peace despite provocations which, in other days, because of their seriousness, could well have engendered war . . .

"Resolute in our determination to respect the right of others and to command the respect for the rights of ourselves, we must keep ourselves adequately strong in self defense."

Thus Roosevelt was determined to speak from a future position of power. America was embarked on an armament race. Admittedly

[75]

it was not enough to cope with the attack on Pearl Harbor that would occur in 1941, but the *Panay* incident prepared the American public for the possibility of war and showed them the necessity for remaining strong.

Of course, America did not know it at the time, but she would have four years, almost to the day, to prepare for Pearl Harbor. News stories and Norman Alley's closely guarded reels helped the American public to understand the government's increasingly war-like attitude.

These newsreel films were complete in almost every detail, except for the missing 30 feet, when they finally were shown to the American public. Audiences sat stunned as the dramatic scenes flashed in front of them. Each of the ship's many flags were caught by the cameras. Instead of smoke and haze, the films verified a clear, sunny day with excellent visibility — a perfect day for an aerial attack.

Both Universal's Norman Alley and Movietone's Eric Mayell had stayed aboard to take shots of the wreckage and had therefore missed the machine-gunning of the rescue boats. They had also missed the Japanese launches' machine-gunning of the *Panay* after the abandon ship order because they buried their cameras in mud to avoid capture. But they had missed little else.

Alley's shots of the actual raiding planes and Mayell's pictures of the bombing of the tanker gave the American public all the proof they needed of Japanese intentions. Alley's shot of a Chinese woman in bombed-out Nanking, her two children beside her, and her husband dead at her feet, stunned viewers almost as much as the valiant defense put up by *Panay*'s gunners. Movietone's nine-minute release and Alley's twenty-three-minute three-reeler thus went down in history as two of the world's most remarkable documentaries.

[76]

Throughout the country the average American's anger began to rise. The *"Panay* incident," as it came to be known, brought war again to the American doorstep. Diplomats, wise in the way of greedy rulers, anticipated the coming holocaust. The American ambassador to Japan foresaw the possible results. Grew said that settlement of the *Panay* affair might well be only temporary, and that Japanese-American relations were resting on treacherous sands.

Four years later proved how correct he had been.

Index

About the author

Born in Parkersburg, West Virginia, Rear Admiral Joseph B. Icenhower, U.S.N. (Ret.) graduated from the U.S. Naval Academy in 1936. As commanding officer on submarines during World War II, he was awarded several medals for outstanding bravery. He is the author of many books.

DATE DUE

FEB 2 0 '79	NOV 1 7 1998	
FEB 8 '79		DEC 1 8 1998
MAR 2 9 1979		
APR 1 9 1979		
MAR 2 0 1980		
NOV 1 8 1980		
JAN 0 8 1981		
FEB 4 1982		
MAR 4 1982		
NOV 1 1 1983		
MAR 2 7 1986		
MAR 1 6 1993		
OCT 0 7 1998		